Edward D. (Edward Duffield) Neill

Occurrences in and around Fort Snelling

From 1819 to 1840

Edward D. (Edward Duffield) Neill

Occurrences in and around Fort Snelling
From 1819 to 1840

ISBN/EAN: 9783337189167

Printed in Europe, USA, Canada, Australia, Japan

Cover: Foto ©ninafisch / pixelio.de

More available books at **www.hansebooks.com**

OCCURRENCES IN AND AROUND

FORT SNELLING,

FROM 1819 TO 1840.

BY E. D. NEILL.

FOR nearly fifty years Fort Snelling has been well known for the beauty and prominence of its situation, at the junction of the Minnesota and Mississippi rivers.

Recently a portion of its outer wall has fallen, caused by excavations for the track of a railroad, and, under the advancing and resistless pressure of modern civilization, it may be, that within a generation, not one stone will be left on another. In anticipation of its disappearance, it is the object of this article to narrate some of the incidents connected with the Fort and the vicinity, previous to the organization of Minnesota.

After the cession of Louisiana to the United States, President Jefferson sent an exploring expedition under Lieut. Z. M. Pike to the Upper Mississippi. On the 23d of September, 1805, on the island which is called by his name, at the mouth of the Minnesota, Pike held a conference with the Sioux, and obtained a grant of lands for military purposes, nine miles square, at the mouth of the St. Croix, also from below the confluence of the Minnesota and Mississippi, and up the latter, to include the Falls of Saint Anthony, extending nine miles on each side of the river.

The war with Great Britian, and other causes, delayed

the establishment of a post on the Upper Mississippi for several years; but on the 10th of February, 1819, John C. Calhoun, then Secretary of War, issued an order for the 5th Regiment of Infantry to rendezvous at Detroit, preparatory to proceeding to the Mississippi to garrison or establish military posts, and the headquarters of the regiment was directed to be at the fort to be located at the mouth of the Minnesota, then St. Peter's river.

It was not until the 17th of September, that Lieut.-Col. Leavenworth, with a detachment of troops, reached this point, the keel-boats having been much delayed by the very low stage of water.

A cantonment was first established at New Hope, near Mendota, not far from the ferry. During the winter of 1819–20, forty of the soldiers died from scurvy. In the spring of 1820 J. B. Faribault came up from Prairie du Chien with Leavenworth's horses, and made his permanent home in Minnesota. Through his influence with the commanding officer, he obtained a *quasi* grant from the Indians of Pike's Island, but after an investigation of the circumstances, the government refused to confirm it.

On the 5th of May, Leavenworth crossed the Minnesota, and established a summer camp near the spring, above the military graveyard, which was called "Cold Water." The relations of Colonel Leavenworth with the Indian Agent at this time were not as harmonious as they might have been. The former was disposed to distribute medals and presents, and assumed duties that had not been delegated. Gov. Cass, returning from his tour to the Upper Mississippi, stopped at Camp Coldwater, and seems to have appreciated the Agent's position. The actions of the Colonel led to the following letter from Major Taliaferro:—

CAMP ST. PETERS, July 30, 1820.

DEAR SIR: As it is now understood that I am the Agent for Indian Affairs in this country, and you are about to leave the

Upper Mississippi, in all probability in the course of a month or two, I beg leave to suggest, for the sake of a general understanding with the Indian tribes in this country, that any medals you may possess would, by being turned over to me, cease to be a topic of remark among the different bands of Indians under my direction. I will pass to you any voucher that may be required, and I beg leave to observe also that my progress in influence is much impeded in consequence of their frequent intercourse with the garrison. The more they become familiarized to our strength in this country, the less apt they are to respect either the Agent or his Government. On reflection you will doubtless think me correct.

I am, sir, very respectfully,

Your friend and obedient servant,

LAWR. TALIAFERRO,

Indian Agent Upper Mississippi.

Col. H. LEAVENWORTH,

Commanding 5th Infantry, Camp Coldwater.

This disastrous effect of the unrestricted intercourse of Indians, with the soldiers of the garrison, was forcibly exhibited a few days subsequent to the date of this letter.

On the third of August, Mahgossau, a chief called by the whites "Old Bustard," accompanied by another Indian, visited Camp Coldwater, and was presented with "fire water." While on his return to the Agency, still kept at the first cantonment, his comrade stabbed him. The occurrence called forth the following note:—

INDIAN AGENCY, ST. PETERS, August 5, 1820.

DEAR SIR: His Excellency Gov. Cass, during his visit to this Post, remarked to me that the Indians in this quarter were spoiled, and at the same time said that they should not be permitted to enter the Camp. I beg leave to suggest to you the propriety of his remark, by an observance of which my influence may be facilitated and the government respected. An unpleasant affair has lately taken place. I mean the stabbing of the old chief Mahgossau by his comrade. This was caused, doubtless, by an anxiety to obtain the chief's whiskey. I beg, therefore, that no whiskey whatever be given to any Indian, unless it be through their proper Agent. While an overplus of whiskey thwarts the beneficent and humane policy of the Government, it entails misery upon the Indians, and endangers their lives as well as those of their own people.

Very respectfully, your obedient servant,

LAWR. TALIAFERRO, Indian Agent.

Col. H. LEAVENWORTH, Commanding 5th Infantry.

A few days after this correspondence, Colonel Josiah Snelling arrived, and relieved Leavenworth. His presence infused system and energy among men and officers. On the 10th of September the corner stone of Fort St. Anthony was laid. The barracks were at first log structures. During the summer of 1820 a party of the Sisseton Sioux killed on the Missouri Isadore Poupon, a half-breed, and Joseph Andrews, a Canadian, two men in the employ of a fur company. As soon as the intelligence reached the Agent, Major Taliaferro, trade with the Sioux was interdicted until the guilty were surrendered. Finding that they were deprived of blankets, powder, and tobacco, a council was held at Big Stone Lake, and one of the murderers, and the aged father of another, agreed to go down and surrender themselves.

On the 12th of November, escorted by friends and relatives, they approached the post. Halting for a brief period, they formed and marched in solemn procession to the centre of the parade ground. In advance was a Sisseton, bearing a British flag; next came the murderer, and the old man who had offered himself as an atonement for his son, with their arms pinioned, and large wooden splinters thrust through the flesh above the elbow, indicating their contempt for pain; and in the rear followed friends chanting the death-song.

After burning the British flag in front of the sentinels of the Fort, they formally delivered the prisoners. The murderer was sent under guard to St. Louis, and the old man detained as a hostage.

The first white women in Minnesota were the wives of army officers. Mrs. Snelling accompanied her husband, and a few days after her arrival at Mendota, a daughter was born, and after a brief existence of thirteen months, died and was buried in the graveyard of the fort. It was the first interment, and the stone which marks its remains can still be seen.

The wife of Captain Clark, the commissary of the post, arrived in 1820, with an infant, born at Fort Winnebago, Wisconsin, who still lives, a resident of Minnesota, and the honored wife of the quiet, efficient, and unassuming Major General Van Cleve.

Mrs. Gooding, the wife of Captain Gooding, remained at the post until 1821, when her husband resigned, and became the sutler of Prairie du Chien.

The year 1821 was occupied by the military in the construction of the fort, and by Major Taliaferro, the Agent, in dissipating the prejudices of the Indians, instilled by British traders.

On the 12th of September a party of Sissetons visited the Agent, and the spokesman said:—

"We are glad to find your door open to-day, my father. The Indians, you see, are like the wild dogs of the prairie. When they stop at night, they lie down in the open air, and rise with the sun and pursue their journey. I applied for the other murderer of the white men of the Missouri, but in bringing him down, the fear of being hung induced him to stab himself to death."

Early in August, a young and intelligent mixed blood, Alexis Bailly, left the fort for the Red River settlement, with a drove of thirty or forty cattle.

On the 1st of October, Major Taliaferro and some of the officers of the fort, and Mrs. Captain Gooding, rode up to the Falls of Saint Anthony, to visit the government mill, being constructed under the supervision of Lieut. McCabe. Two weeks later, Col. Snelling, Lieut. Baxley, Mrs. Gooding, and Major Taliaferro went to Prairie du Chien in the keelboat "Saucy Jack."

Early in January, 1822, Alexis Bailly, Col. Robert Dickson, and Messrs. Laidlaw and Mackenzie arrived at the Prairie from Selkirk Settlement. While here, the Indian Agent learned that at a saw-mill on the Black River, built by Hardin Perkins, a foreign subject, named J. B. Mayraud, was trading without a license, and on the 2d of February, he sent Thomas McNair to seize his goods. The notorious Joseph Rolette, sen., attempted to frustrate the plan by sending Alexis Bailly to give warning. On the same day that McNair was sent to Black River, M. Dousman was authorized to take possession of the stores of Montreville, trading with the Indians above Lake Pepin.

From that time the old British traders did not leave a stone unturned to effect the removal of Major Taliaferro, as he could not be coaxed nor intimidated to wink at the plans for fleecing the ignorant Indians.

In the fall of 1822, Fort St. Anthony was sufficiently completed to admit of its occupancy by the troops.

In the spring of 1823, it was proved that it was practicable to navigate the Mississippi with steamboats as far as the Minnesota River. The Virginia, a steamer one hundred and eighteen feet in length and twenty-two in width, commanded by Captain Crawford, on the 10th of May made its appearance at the Fort, and was received with a salute. Among the passengers were Major Biddle, Lt. Russell, Taliaferro, the Indian Agent, and Beltrami, an Italian refugee and traveller, with letters of introduction to Col. Snelling and family. On the 3d of July, Major Long, of the Topographical Engineers, arrived at the Fort, at the head of an expedition to explore the Minnesota River, and the region along the northern boundary line of the United States. Beltrami, at the instance of Col. Snelling, was permitted to be one of the exploring party, and Major Taliaferro kindly gave him a horse and equipments. The relations of the Italian to Long did not prove pleasant, and at Pembina, Beltrami separated from the party, and, with a "bois brule" and two Ojibways, proceeded and discovered the northern sources of the Mississippi, and suggested where the western sources would be found, which was verified by Schoolcraft nine years later. About the second week in September, Beltrami returned to the Fort by way of the Mississippi, escorted by forty or fifty Ojibways, and on the 25th departed for New Orleans, where he published his discoveries in the French language.

In the year 1824, the Fort was visited by General Scott, on a tour of inspection, and at his suggestion its name was changed from Fort St. Anthony to Fort Snelling.

The following is an extract from his report to the War Department:—

This work, of which the War Department is in possession of a plan, reflects the highest credit on Col. Snelling, his officers and men. The defences, and for the most part the public storehouses, shops, and quarters being constructed of stone, the whole is likely to endure as long as the post shall remain a frontier one. The cost of erection to the government has only been the amount paid for tools and iron, and the per diem paid to soldiers employed as mechanics.

I wish to suggest to the General-in-Chief, and through him to the War Department, the propriety of calling this work Fort Snelling, as a just compliment to the meritorious officer under whom it has been erected.

The present name [Fort St. Anthony] is foreign to all our associations, and is besides geographically incorrect, as the work stands at the junction of the Mississippi and St. Peter's rivers, eight miles below the great falls of the Mississippi, called after St. Anthony.

In 1824, Major Taliaferro proceeded to Washington, with a delegation of Chippeways and Dahkotahs headed by Little Crow, the grandfather of the chief of the same name, who was engaged in the late horrible massacre of defenceless women and children. The object of the visit was to secure a convocation of all the tribes of the Upper Mississippi at Prairie du Chien, to define their boundary lines and establish friendly relations. When they reached Praire du Chien, Wahnatah, a Yancton chief, and also Wapasha, by the whisperings of mean traders, became disaffected, and wished to turn back. Little Crow, perceiving this, stopped all hesitancy by the following speech:—

"MY FRIENDS: You can do as you please. I am no coward, nor can my ears be pulled about by evil counsels. We are here and should go on, and do some good for our nation. I have taken our Father here [Taliaferro] by the coat-tail, and will follow him until I take by the hand our great American Father."

While on board of a steamer on the Ohio river, Marcpee or the Cloud, in consequence of a bad dream, jumped from the stern of the boat, and was supposed to be drowned, but he swam ashore and made his way to St. Charles, Mo., there to be murdered by some Sacs. The remainder safely arrived in Washington, and accomplished the object of the visit. The Dahkotahs returned by the way of New York, and while there were anxious to pay a visit to certain parties with Wm. Dickson, a half-breed son of Col. Robert Dickson, the trader who led the Indians of the Northwest against the United States in the war of 1812.

After this visit, Little Crow carried a new double-barrelled gun, and said that a medicine man by the name of Peters gave it to him for signing a certain paper, and that he also promised he would send a keelboat full of goods to them. The medicine man referred to was the Rev. Samuel Peters, an Episcopal clergyman, who had made

himself obnoxious during the Revolution by his tory senti-
ments, and was subsequently nominated as Bishop of Vermont.*

Peters asserted that in 1806 he had purchased of the
heirs of Jonathan Carver the right to a tract of land on the
Upper Mississippi, embracing St. Paul, alleged to have
been given to Carver by the Dahkotahs in 1767.

The next year there arrived in one of the keelboats from
Prairie du Chien at Fort Snelling, a box marked for Col.
Robert Dickson. On opening, it was found to contain a
few presents from Mr. Peters to Dickson's Indian wife, a
long letter, and a copy of Carver's alleged grant, written
on parchment.

As early as April 5th, 1825, the steamboat Rufus Put-

* The Rt. Rev. Bishop Chase, Bishop of New Hampshire, in his notes
on the History of the Protestant Episcopal Church in Vermont, says:
"The Rev. Samuel Peters, LL.D., familiarly known among our older
churchmen under the name of 'Bishop Peters,' tells us [see his Life of
Hugh Peters, p. 94], that he was the first clergyman who visited 'Verd
Mont,' as he calls it. This was in October, 1768, when, with a number
of gentlemen, he ascended to one of the Green Mountain peaks, and there,
in sight of Lake Champlain on the west and of Connecticut River on the
east, and stretching his view over interminable forests northward and
southward, proclaimed the name of 'Verd Mont.' After this, as he re-
lates, he passed through most of the settlements, preaching and baptizing
for the space of eight weeks. The number baptized by him, at that early
period, of adults and children, is set down at nearly twelve hundred—a
number very remarkable, certainly, considering the sparseness of the
population."

It is said to be on record that he was *nominated* for colonial Bishop of
Vermont, by some one of the British colonial governors. Accordingly
he went to England to procure consecration, but was rejected. After the
close of the War of the Revolution he revived his claim to the bishopric
of Vermont, and applied to the newly consecrated American Bishops;
but from some cause he failed to make his claims respected, and so never
became Bishop. He was an extreme tory, and spent most of his life in
political intriguery. He died in New York, April 19, 1826, at the age
of ninety years.—*Committee.*

nam, Captain Bates in command, reached the Fort.   Four weeks after she made a second trip with goods for the Columbia Fur Company, and proceeded to Land's End, their trading post on the Minnesota River.

This year was also remarkable for the great convocation of tribes at Prairie du Chien, in the presence of Governors Cass and Clark, at which a definite boundary line between the Chippeways and Dahkotah country was agreed upon.

After the council was over, Mr. Taliaferro and delegation left in three Mackinaw boats, with eighteen voyageurs.   Great sickness prevailed among the Indians.   Before Lake Pepin was reached, a Sisseton chief died.   At Little Crow's village, on the east side of the river, just below the present city of St. Paul, the sickness had so increased that it was necessary to leave one of the boats, and, after much tribulation, on the 30th of August, the remainder of the party reached Fort Snelling.   The Agent appointed Mr. Laidlaw to conduct the Yanctons, Wahpetons, Wahkpacootays, and Sissetons to their homes, but on the way twelve died.

Among the sick Chippeways who died at the mouth of the Sauk River, about the same time, was the wife of Hole-in-the-Day, and the mother of the present chief of that name.

On the 30th of October, seven Indian women, in canoes, were drawn into the rapids above the Falls of St. Anthony. All were saved but a lame girl who was dashed over the Falls, whose body, a month afterwards, was found at Pike's Island, in front of the Fort.

Forty years ago, the means of communication between Fort Snelling and the civilized world were very limited. The mail in the winter was usually carried by soldiers to Prairie du Chien.   On the 26th of January, 1826, there was great joy in the fort, caused by the return from furlough of Lieutenants Baxley and Russell, who brought with them the first mail received for *five* months.   About this period there was also another excitement caused by the seizure of liquors in the trading house of Alexis Bailly, at New Hope, now Mendota.

In February, the monotony of wilderness life was again broken by a duel between two officers of the garrison. On the 23d of this month the officers went down to Faribault's house, a short distance from Carver's Cave, to attend a grand medicine dance. During the month of March, a young son of Lieutenant Melancthon Smith died. Officers and men, preceded by a band of music playing the "Dead March," escorted the remains to their last resting place.

On the 8th of February, Colonel Snelling received the following letter from the Indian Agent:—

DEAR SIR: Agreeably to your request, made a few days since, desiring information as to the most practicable and speedy route to the several trading posts on the Upper Mississippi, also the number of points at which locations have been made for carrying on trade with the Indians, and also any other information deemed pertinent to the subject, that might be in my possession:

I have at length, after a full examination of documents in my office, been enabled to state as follows: The number of locations made by me under the act of Congress of the 26th of May, 1824, on the waters of the Mississippi alone, amount to seven in number, viz., one at the mouth of Chippeway River, one at the Falls of St. Croix, one at Crow Island, one at Sandy Lake, one at Leaf Lake, one at Leech Lake, and one at Red Lake.

My letter to you of the 6th of January last, informs you of the purport of Mr. Prescott's report, and there is no doubt but that the goods and peltries of those Canadians near his house, are liable to and wou d be a lawful seizure, besides the forfeiture of their bonds, in the sum of $500 each, they entering the country to serve as boatswain or interpreter, as the case may be.

Mr. Baker reports one house to be in operation between Crow Island and Sandy Lake, where no location has been made by any Agent of the government. This trader, it appears, was licensed for Red Lake, and permitted to take with him twenty kegs of liquor, but found it better suited his purpose to establish himself as before stated.

There may be some whiskey at Sandy Lake, but no large quantity nearer than the post of the American Fur Company, at the Fond-du-lac, on Lake Superior, which would be too far for troops to march at this advanced season of the winter. I am also informed that the buildings which were erected for the accommodation of our troops while getting timber for the public service last winter, are now occupied by common hands of the American Fur Company, and are no doubt unlawfully engaged in the Indian trade. Traders have no right to station their men at any point, other than at special posts, assigned in their licenses.

As it is not in my power to give a correct statement of the route from this point to the leading locations above on the Mississippi, I have, therefore, procured a faithful Indian as a guide to the first post, Crow Island, where every facility to the other posts will be afforded by Mr. B. F. Baker.

I am fully impressed with the belief that showing a detachment of troops occasionally in the Indian country, on the Upper Mississippi, will have the effect, in a short time, of putting an entire stop to this petty illicit trade, and the bartering of whiskey, which has been carried on for several years past. And it also makes strong impressions on the minds of the Indians. They see that the government can reach them and the traders also at pleasure.

In connection with this letter, we record the locations and names of all the posts within the Agency at that time:—

1. Fort Adams, Lac-qui-parle, house of Columbia Fur Company.
2. Fort Washington, Lac Traverse,   "   "   "   "
3. Fort Columbia, Upper Sand Hills, Cheyenne American "
4. Fort Biddle, Crow Island,   "   "
5. Fort Rush, mouth of Chippeway River,   "   "
6. Fort Union, Traverse des Sioux, Columbia   "   "
7. Fort Factory, near Fort Snelling, on the St. Peter's.
8. Fort Barbour, Falls of St. Croix, Columbia Fur Company.
9. Fort Calhoun, Leech Lake,   American   "   "
10. Fort Bolivar, Leaf Lake,   Columbia   "   "

11. Fort Pike, Red Lake, American Fur Company.
12. Fort Rice, Devil's Lake,   "   "   "
13. Fort Greene, below Big Stone Lake, American Fur Company.
14. Fort Southard, Forks of Red Cedar River, American Fur Company.
15. Fort Lewis, Little Rapids (St. Peter's), American Fur Company.
16. Fort Confederation, second forks Des Moines River, Columbia Fur Company.
17. Fort Benton, Sandy Lake, American Fur Company.

During the months of February and March, in the year 1826, snow fell to the depth of two or three feet, and there was great suffering among the Indians. On one occasion thirty lodges of Sisseton and other Sioux were overtaken by a snow storm on a large prairie. The storm continued for three days, and provisions grew scarce, for the party were seventy in number. At last the stronger men, with a few pairs of snow-shoes in their possession, started for a trading post one hundred miles distant. They reached their destination half alive, and the traders sympathizing, sent four Canadians with supplies for those left behind. After great toil they reached the scene of distress and found many dead; and, what was more horrible, the living feeding on the corpses of their relatives. A mother had eaten her dead child, and a portion of her own father's arms. The shock to her nervous system was so great that she lost her reason. Her name was Tash-u-no-ta, and she was both young and good-looking. One day in September 1829, while at Fort Snelling, she asked Captain Jouett if he knew which was the best portion of a man to eat, at the same time taking him by the collar of his coat. He replied with great astonishment, "No," and she then said "the arms." She then asked for a piece of his servant to eat, as she was nice and fat. A few days after this, she dashed herself from the bluffs near Fort Snelling, into the river. Her body was found just above the mouth of the Minnesota, and decently interred by the Agent.

The spring of 1826 was very backward. On the 20th of March snow fell to the depth of one or one and a half feet on a level, and drifted in heaps from six to fifteen feet in height. On the 5th of April, early in the day, there was a violent snow storm, and the ice was still thick in the river. During the storm, flashes of lightning were seen and thunder heard. On the 10th, the thermometer was four degrees above zero. On the 14th, there was a rain, and on the next day the St. Peter's river broke up, but the ice in the Mississippi remained firm. On the 21st, at noon, the ice began to move, and carried away Mr. Faribault's houses on the east side of the river. For several days the river was twenty feet above low-water mark, and all the houses on low lands were swept off. On the 2d of May the steamboat Lawrence, Capt. Reeder, arrived.

Major Taliaferro had inherited several slaves, that he used to hire to officers of the garrison. On the 31st of March, his negro boy William was employed by Col. Snelling, the latter agreeing to clothe him. About this time William attempted to shoot a hawk, but instead shot a small boy, named Henry McCullum, and nearly killed him. In May, Captain Plympton of the 5th Infantry wished to purchase his negro woman Eliza, but he refused, as it was his intention ultimately to free his slaves. Another of his negro girls, Harriet, was married at the Fort, the Major performing the ceremony, to the now historic Dred Scott, who was then a slave of Surgeon Emerson.

The only person that ever purchased a slave was Alexis Bailly, who bought a man from Major Garland. The Sioux at first had no prejudices against negroes. They called them "black Frenchmen," and placing their hands on their woolly heads would laugh heartily.

The following is a list of the steamboats that had arrived at Fort Snelling up to May 26, 1826:—

1. Virginia, May 10, 1823.
2. Neiville.
3. Putnam, April 2, 1825.
4. Mandan.
5. Indiana.
6. Lawrence, May 2, 1826.
7. Sciota.
8. Eclipse.
9. Josephine.
10. Fulton.
11. Red Rover.
12. Black Rover.
13. Warrior.
14. Enterprise.
15. Volant.

The subjoined was written by Colonel Snelling to Major Taliaferro, while the latter was on a visit to the Sioux of the Upper Minnesota:—

FORT SNELLING, August 26, 1826.

DEAR SIR: Your letter of the 24th was received last evening. I have directed Capt. Watkins to take twenty days rations; it will be better to have a surplus than a deficiency. Col. Croghan has been here, and departed very well satisfied. Mr. Marsh accompanied him, and left a letter for you, which I now send. It seems that Mr. Secretary Barbour took no other notice of your letter than to send it to Gov. Cass, and he gave it to Marsh, and "*so we go.*" I have no serious apprehensions for the safety of Fort Crawford, but the reports afloat were of such an imposing character that I thought it my duty to reinforce it. If it had fallen for want of aid, I should have lost my military reputation forever. I trust that you will agree with me that Capt. Wilcox was a good selection for the command. Wabasha is said to have agreed to join the confederacy, if the Sioux of the St. Peters would do it, and they have declined. We have no mail, nor news. Your affairs go on well under Mr. L., who is a general favorite. My family is about as usual. Joseph's wound is doing well. Madam desires to be sincerely and cordially remembered to you. Capt. Garland is here, with a very interesting family. Remember me to Lt. Jamieson.

Truly your friend,

Major L. TALIAFERRO,   J. SNELLING.
Indian Agent for the Sioux of the St. Peters.

During the fall of 1826 all the troops at Fort Crawford were brought up to Fort Snelling, rendering the garrison very full.

On the night of the 28th of May, 1827, while Flat Mouth, Chief of the Pillagers, and a detachment of the Sandy Lake Indians were quietly encamped in front of the Agency House, and under the guns of the Fort, nine Sioux attacked them, wounding eight of the party. The Sioux were immediately notified that as they had insulted the flag of the United States they must make ample satisfaction. On the next day they delivered nine of the assailants, and two of them were immediately shot. On the 31st, two more were delivered up, and met with a similar fate.

Among the wounded Chippeways was a little girl ten years old, who had been shot through the thighs. Surgeon McMahon made every effort to save her life, but without avail.

After the removal of the troops from Fort Crawford to Fort Snelling, the Winnebagoes became more and more insolent, and in the month of March, 1827, they attacked the camp of a half-breed at Painted Rock Creek, on the Iowa side of the river, above the prairie, and killed the whole family.

About the same time two keelboats, with provisions, on their way to Fort Snelling, had been ordered to land at Wapasha's village, by his band of Sioux, but the crew, by preserving a bold mien, were not molested.

On their return, while about 50 miles above Prairie du Chien, they were attacked by some Winnebagoes, maddened by liquor obtained from Joseph Rolette. Joseph Snelling, a son of the Colonel, who was a passenger on one of the boats, in a letter to his father, said that the front boat, which was a few miles in advance of the other, was attacked in the evening, and pierced with hundreds of bullets. The Indians then boarded the boat, and attempted to run her ashore, but by the signal bravery of the crew they were driven off. The rear boat was also attacked, but after several rounds were fired, they desisted.

Murders were also committed near Prairie du Chien, and the panic-stricken settlers had taken refuge in Fort Crawford.

As soon as the intelligence was received, on the evening of July 9th, Col. Snelling started in keelboats with four companies to protect Fort Crawford, and on the 17th of August four more companies of 5th Infantry left under Major Fowle.

After an absence of six weeks, the soldiers returned to Fort Snelling without firing a gun at the enemy. General Atkinson quieted the Winnebagoes by the execution of their two prominent warriors, Red Bird and Wekaw, who surrendered.

During the fall of this year, the 5th Regiment of infantry was ordered to Jefferson Barracks, and after their arrival at that post, Colonel Snelling proceeded to Washington to settle some accounts, and, while in that city, was seized with inflammation of the brain and died.

On the 15th of February, 1828, Alexis Bailly, trader at New Hope, now Mendota, applied for the establishment of a new trading post for the Wahpaykootays, on the Cannon River.

During the winter of 1828, Duncan Grahame and Jean Brunet began to cut timber on the Chippeway River, as Perkins & Co. had done in 1823. This act being considered an infraction of the law, Duncan Campbell was sent to visit the parties. His instructions were in these words: —

INDIAN AGENCY, ST. PETERS,
February 13, 1828.

SIR: The enclosed letter you will, on reaching the Chippeway River, deliver to Mr. Duncan Grahame, who is reported to be engaged in trade on that river.

You will take every possible means to inform yourself of this fact, and report the circumstances to this office. It is also desirable that you ascertain the number of persons engaged in procuring timber at the same place, and particularly at what distance below the Falls of the Chippeway.   *   *   *   *   Mr. Quinn will accompany you on the present expedition, as it is unsafe, from the severity of the season, to proceed alone.

During the month of June, Samuel Gibson, a drover from Missouri, lost his way while driving cattle to Fort Snelling, and he abandoned them near Lac-qui-parle. The trader there, Mr. Renville, took charge of them, and sixty-four head were subsequently sold by the Indian Agent's order, for $750, and the money forwarded to the unfortunate drover.

The winter, spring, and summer of 1829 were exceedingly dry. For ten months the average monthly fall of rain and snow was one inch. Vegetation was more backward than it had been for ten years, and navigation during the summer was almost impossible.

On the evening of July 27th, Lieut. Reynolds arrived with a keelboat of supplies, but one-half of the load had to be left at Pine Bend, before the boat could pass the bar in that vicinity, and sixty days were occupied in coming from St. Louis. The arrival was most opportune, as the garrison were eating their last barrel of flour. This summer Hazen Mooers came down from Lake Traverse, with one hundred and twenty-six packs of furs, valued at twelve thousand dollars.

It was in this year that the first attempt, in the present century, was made to establish missions in Minnesota.

In a journal kept at the Fort, under the date of Monday, Aug. 31st, is this entry:—

"The Rev. Mr. Coe and Stephens reported to be on their way to this post—members of the Presbyterian church, looking out for suitable places to make missionary establishments for the Sioux and Chippeways, found schools, instruct in agriculture and the arts, etc."

On the 1st of September these clergymen arrived and became the guests of the Indian Agent, with whom they had frequent conversations on the propriety of forming a colony in the Chippeway country, and also at the Falls of St. Anthony, for the Sioux. The Agent explained what steps he had taken toward forming schools.

On Sunday, September 6th, Rev. Mr. Coe preached twice, and the next evening held a prayer meeting at the quarters of the commanding officer. He also preached on the next Sunday, and on Monday, the 14th, he and his companion, with a guide, started on horseback for the St. Croix River. Mr. Taliaferro had already commenced an agricultural establishment on Lake Calhoun, which he called Eatonville, and he was very glad to meet with any who had the welfare of the Indian in view, as the following letter shows:—

INDIAN AGENCY, ST. PETERS,
September 8th, 1829.

REV. SIR: It having been represented to me by the Rev. Alvan Coe, that it is very desirable on the part of the Board of Missions of the Presbyterian Church to form an establishment at this post, and also within the heart of the Chippeway country bordering on the Upper Mississippi, for the purpose of agriculture, schools, and the development of the light and truths of the Christian religion to the unhappy aborigines of this vast wilderness.

As my views fully accord in every material point with those of Messrs. Coe and Stephens, I can, in truth, assure the Board through you, Sir, of my determination heartily to co-operate with them in any and every measure that may be calculated to ensure success in the highly interesting and important objects to which the attention of the society has been so happily directed.

I have recommended to the government to appoint a special sub-agent, to reside at Gull Lake, to superintend the general concerns of the most warlike and respectable portion of all the Chippeways of the Mississippi and its tributary waters above Lake Pepin, thereby to lessen their visits to this Agency, it being desirable to prevent their coming in contact too often with their old enemies the Sioux.

Should the society form a missionary establishment on the waters of the St. Croix, some of which communicate with Rum River of the Mississippi, and a special agent or sub-agent, the influence of whom might be necessary to the more efficient operations of the missionary families there located, I have no doubt but that the government would be willing to appoint one for the special duty, if represented by the society, accompanied by explanatory views on the subject.

As to an establishment for the Sioux of this Agency, it would be in the power of the society to commence operations, without much expense, at the Falls of St. Anthony, where there is a good grist and saw mill, with suitable buildings, at present going to decay for the want of occupants. I would cheerfully turn over my at present infant colony of agriculturists, together with their implements and horses, etc., to such an establishment.

I have the honor to be, Sir,

Respectfully your most obedient servant,

LAW. TALIAFERRO,

Indian Agent at St. Peters,

Upper Mississippi.

REV. JOSHUA T. RUSSELL, Secretary Board of Missions Presbyterian Church, Philadelphia, Pa.

Early in September, Surgeon R. C. Wood left the fort on a visit to Prairie du Chien, and on the last of the month he returned in an open boat, with a youthful bride by his side, the eldest daughter of Col. Zachary Taylor. How wonderful are the changes of a generation! Col. Taylor lived to become the President of the United States. Dr. R. C. Wood, his son-in-law, is now the Asst. Surgeon General of the United States, while Jefferson Davis, another son-in-law, under the influence of ambition, has become President of the States in rebellion, and John Wood, a grandson of

Taylor, is the Commander of the Tallahassee, the noted rebel privateer.

In the year 1830, Col. Taylor was one of the Commissioners appointed to hold another treaty with the Indians at Prairie du Chien. For some reason the traders threw obstacles in the way, which called forth a letter from "Old Zach," with these words, "Take the American Fur Company in the aggregate, and they are the greatest scoundrels the world ever knew."

This year there were so many drunken and licentious Indians lounging around the Fort that the following order was issued by Capt. Gale, the officer in command:—

HEADQUARTERS, FORT SNELLING, June 17, 1830.

The Commanding Officer has within a few mornings past discovered Indian women leaving the garrison immediately after reveille. The practice of admitting Indians into the Fort to remain during the night is strictly prohibited. No officer will hereafter pass any Indian or Indians into the garrison without special permission from the Commanding Officer. It is made the duty of the officer of the day to see that this order is strictly enforced.

By order of

CAPT. GALE.

E. R. WILLIAMS, Lt. and Adj't.

The next day after this order was read Capt. Gale received the following letter from Major Taliaferro:—

AGENCY HOUSE, ST. PETERS, June 18th, 1830.

SIR: Since my request to you of yesterday to co-operate with me in endeavoring to counteract the views of the traders near this post, by excluding all Indians from the Fort, I have become more fully acquainted with other facts of a nature calculated to ensure their success in preventing the Indians from attending the contemplated treaty at Prairie du Chien this summer.

Penition's band yesterday received by the hands of one of his nephews a keg of whiskey, and this same band has been kept through the instrumentality of the traders in a state of continual drunkenness for some time past.

No man can be made better acquainted with these facts than myself. I shall place Mr. Farribault's bond in suit, as also Mr. Culbertson's, the moment it becomes fairly developed as to the course which has been pursued by them respectively. I have sent confidential persons to all the villages to see how the Indians get their whiskey and from whom, and what number are found drunk in each.

I have again to request that no Indians be permitted to enter the Fort for purposes of trade, as they have done for some time past, for they become insolent, lazy, and begin to attempt to take a stand independent of me; consequently nothing short of their entire exclusion from the Fort will effectually correct the evil now complained of.

Mr. Campbell has just returned from his expedition to the several bands of Sioux. On his passage through their country they, upon learning my message, were willing to attend the treaty, but on his return all that he saw refused to accompany him to this place, on the ground that an Indian messenger had passed just after him stating that the Sioux ought not to go down to the Prairie, for if they did they would be turned over to the Sacs and Foxes by the white people. This report naturally caused the whole of the band to disperse—their chiefs setting the example. Again, others state that as they can get plenty of whiskey from their traders and a little tobacco, that they had no occasion to go anywhere, and would not go—so that in the brief space of nine months my influence with most of the bands has been greatly impaired, in consequence of the quantities of whiskey which have been given them by the traders. Consequently the humane policy of the Government in regard to these deluded people has thus unhappily been interfered with, and this too at a time when it was all important for them to have accepted of its munificence and mediation.

The disappointment and embarrassment which will be caused the Commissioners by the refusal of the Sioux to attend may be more easily imagined than described, as the treaty cannot well go on without them, they being mainly concerned.

I have the honor to be, very respectfully,

your most ob't serv't,

LAW. TALIAFERRO,

Indian Agent at St. Peters.

Capt. J. H. GALE, 1st Infantry, Comd'g Fort Snelling.

Notwithstanding the impediments thrown in the way, some of the Sioux attended the congress of tribes, and the M'dewakantonwans, in a treaty made at that time, bestowed on their half-breed relatives the country about Lake Pepin known as the "half-breed tract."

After the agent and delegation of Sioux went to Prairie du Chien, a nephew of Little Crow, with fifteen or twenty of the Kaposia band, went to the St. Croix and killed Cadotte, a half-breed, and three or four Chippeways.

Before daylight, on the morning of August 14th, 1830, a sentinel discovered the Indian council house on fire, and gave the alarm, but it was soon entirely consumed. The afternoon before, some drunken Indians came over from Mr. Bailly's trading house, and used abusive language.

On the 11th of September, Mrs. Faribault's brother, an Indian, came to the Agent, and voluntarily informed him that his uncle, who married Wapasha's daughter, was the person who burned the council house.

This year the agricultural colony of Sioux at Lake Calhoun, named Eatonville, was under the superintendence of Philander Prescott, who was murdered by the Sioux in the massacre of 1862.

During the year 1831, there was another arrival of emigrants from Selkirk's settlement. On the 25th of July, twenty of those unfortunate colonists came to the Fort, having been informed that the United States would give them farming implements and land near the post.

Joseph R. Brown this year had a trading house at Land's End, a mile above the Fort, on the Minnesota.

About the last of July, forty Sauks passed into the Sioux country, between the head waters of the Cannon and Blue Earth Rivers, where they met and killed several Sioux, at a place called Cintagah, or Grey Tail, not far from where the Sauks and Sissetons had fought in 1822 and 1823.

During this summer, Captain W. R. Jouett was in command of Fort Snelling.

On the 17th of August, Rocque and his son arrived at the Fort, twenty-six days in coming from Prairie du Chien. Rendered obtuse by whiskey, or some other cause, they crossed the Mississippi at Hastings, and ascended the St. Croix, and were fifteen days lost. Meeting some Chippeways at last, they were turned back and shown the right course.

On the 18th of September, Messrs. Dallam, Brisbois, and Joseph R. Brown arrived, having come through from Prairie du Chien by land, an unusual thing at that time.

Although Illinois and Wisconsin settlers were much alarmed in 1832 by the Black Hawk war, there was comparative quiet in the vicinity of Fort Snelling. A few of Wapasha's band united with the whites, and assisted in capturing the fugitives after the battle of Bad Axe.

The first steamboat that arrived at Fort Snelling this year was the Versailles, on May 12, and she was succeeded by the Enterprise, on June 27.

Eatonville colony, on Lake Calhoun, which commenced with twelve Indians, had increased to one hundred and twenty-five, and a good deal of corn was planted.

During the summer, the Sioux found the corpse of a white man near the second fork of the Des Moines River. He was tall, light-haired, dressed in a blue coat, black silk vest, and grayish pantaloons. The Indians took his watch, and about twenty dollars in silver, to Alexander Faribault.

On the 16th of June, Wm. Carr and three drovers arrived at the Fort from Missouri, with eighty head of cattle, and six horses for the use of the troops.

At the urgent solicitation of Mr. Aitkin, the trader, in this year Mr. Ayer, now of Belle Prairie, went to Sandy Lake and opened a mission school for Chippeway children. In 1833 the Rev. W. T. Boutwell, who now resides near Stillwater, established a mission station at Leech Lake.

In the year 1834, Samuel W. and Gideon H. Pond arrived, and offered their services for the benefit of the Sioux, and were sent out to the Agent's agricultural colony on Lake Calhoun. This year also, Henry H. Sibley took charge of trading post at Mendota.

During the month of May, 1835, the Rev. Mr. Williamson, M. D., arrived at Fort Snelling, with his family and assistants, to establish a Sioux mission, and, on the second Sabbath in June, a Presbyterian church was organized in one of the company rooms of the Fort, and the sacrament of the Lord's Supper was administered to twenty-two persons, and Captain, now Colonel, Gustavus Loomis, of the army, was elected one of the session of the church.

In the year 1835, Major J. L. Bean commenced the survey of the Sioux and Chippeway boundary line, under the treaty of 1825. A military escort, under Lt. Wm. Storer, accompanied him, and he proceeded as far as Otter Tail Lake, but the Indians were very troublesome, and constantly pulled up the stakes.

Alexis Bailly, having been found guilty of furnishing Indians with whiskey, was forced to leave the post in June, with his family, and Mr. Sibley became his successor at Mendota.

On the 23d of June, Dr. Williamson and family, and Alexander G. Huggins, mission farmer, left the Fort for Lac-qui-parle, in company with Joseph Renville, Sr.

The next day a long-expected steamboat, the Warrior,

arrived with supplies and a pleasure party. Among the passengers were Captain Day and Lieut. Beech, of the army, Catlin, the artist, and wife, General G. W. Jones, J. Farnsworth, Mrs. Felix St. Vrain, Misses Farnsworth, Crow, Johnson, and others.

On the 3d of July, Major Taliaferro, as justice of the peace, united in marriage Hippolite Provost and Margaret Brunell.

Colonel Kearney, with a detachment of 200 dragoons, passed through the southern part of Minnesota during this month.

On the 16th, the Warrior again arrived at the Fort, and among the passengers were Gen. Robert Patterson, sister and daughter, from Philadelphia. On the 27th, Catlin, the painter, left in a bark canoe, with one soldier, for Prairie du Chien. On the last day of July, a train of Red River emigrants arrived, with some fifty or sixty head of cattle, and twenty or twenty-five horses. Lieut. Ogden, Rev. Mr. Stevens, of Lake Harriet, and Mr. Sibley, purchased some of the horses. Including this party, since 1821, four hundred and eighty-nine persons from Selkirk Colony had arrived at the Fort, while a few, Abraham Perry and others, became farmers in the vicinity. The majority went down to Galena, Vevay, and other points in Illinois and Indiana.

On the 29th of July the Indian Agent married Sophia Perry to a Mr. Godfrey.

Michael Kilcole, an Irishman, and Joseph Vespuli, on their way from Red River, had their three yoke of oxen stolen by the Little Rapids Indians. As they had large families, Major Taliaferro circulated a subscription paper in their behalf, and obtained the following names and sums:—

Major Bliss, $5; Law. Taliaferro, $3; Major Loomis, $3; Capt. Day, $2; B. F. Baker, $2; N. W. Kittson, $1; Lieut. Ogden, $2.

If the Indians had not been made.drunk by the whiskey of unprincipled traders, the robbery would not have been committed.

On the 12th of September, the geologist, Featherston-haugh, arrived. His actions were those of a conceited, ill-bred Englishman, and the book he afterwards published in London, called "A Canoe Voyage up the Minnay Sotor," proved that he was destitute of the instincts of a refined gentleman.

On the 26th of November, Col. Stambaugh, the new sutler for the post, arrived.

The following conversation took place at the headquarters of Major Bliss, on December 7th:—

Major Bliss said, "It was his opinion that a treaty was in contemplation with the Sioux for a cession of land, a large body east of the Mississippi, governed by the bound-ary line between the tribes."

To which the Indian Agent replied:—

"I feel confident there is and has been such a plan in contemplation, although never officially made known to me, but the main object of such a purchase would be to place the Winnebagoes on the west and not east of the Mississippi. Therefore if a treaty be in contemplation at all, it will have for its object the purchase of all the Sioux country, from the cession of 1830, to strike a point from the Red Cedar on to the head waters of the Terre Bleu River, thence to the waters of the River des Canons, and following said river to its mouth; thence with the Missis-sippi River to the line of cession of 1830; or it may be varied so as to touch the River des Moines, Terre Bleu and Cannon Rivers."

Major Bliss added: "I hear many letters have been written for the purpose of effecting the object we speak of, and I shall not be surprised to see a commissioner arrive here next spring."

The Agent replied to this: "I do not know but such a treaty might take place. It is desirable, on the part of the traders of the American Fur Company, that a treaty should be had with the Sioux. The treaty of 1830 first indicated a disposition to cause the United States to pay them for lost credits. I then defeated their object, for I view the allowance of all such claims as a fraud committed upon the Treasury, although legalized by a treaty. The company are much opposed to me on this ground and fear me, and would be glad to have me out of the country. I know too much, and they are fully aware of my independence. I am determined at some future day, Major, to address the President. He abhors iniquity and deception, and he will protect me."

In the month of February, 1836, Fanny, daughter of Abraham Perry, who had emigrated from Selkirk Settlement, was married to Charles Mousseau, being the fifth couple that had been united in marriage by Mr. Taliaferro.

The winter of 1836 proved very severe to cattle. J. B. Faribault lost twenty head, Joseph R. Brown seven, H. H. Sibley seven, L. Taliaferro three, and Joseph Perry ten.

The first steamboat that arrived in 1836 was the Missouri Fulton, on the 8th of May. Major Bliss left in this boat, and Col. Davenport succeeded as commanding officer of the Fort.

On the 29th of May, the steamboat Frontier, Captain Harris, was at the Fort, the second arrival of the season.

On June 1, the Palmyra came, with some thirty ladies and gentlemen passengers. On the 2d of July the St. Peters came up and landed supplies. Among the passengers was Mr. Nicollet, the French astronomer, and several ladies from St. Louis, on a pleasure tour. Mr. Nicollet, who had come for scientific purposes, was kindly furnished with a room in Mr. Taliaferro's house, and a friendship was formed that lasted until the death of the former. The

Indian Agent has the following entry in his Journal, under date of July 12:—

"Mr. Nicollet, on a visit to the post for scientific research, and at present in my family, has shown me the late work of Henry R. Schoolcraft, on the discovery of the source of the Mississippi, which claim is ridiculous in the extreme."

On the 17th, Duncan Campbell, Sr., arrived from the foot of Lake Pepin, and reported that all but twenty-seven of Wapasha's band had died from smallpox.

On the 27th, Nicollet left the Agency for the sources of the Mississippi. Just before his departure he gave Mr. Taliaferro an original letter of Washington to Elias Boudinot, dated August 24, 1795, and giving reasons for not attending the funeral of Mr. Bradford.

On the 30th of July, a party of mounted Sac and Fox Indians killed twenty-four Winnebagoes on Root River. They were descending the stream on their way to La Crosse, and were completely surprised.

On the 12th of September, at the house of Oliver Cratte, near the Fort, James Wells, subsequently a member of the Minnesota Legislature, was united in marriage to Jane Graham, a daughter of Duncan Graham. The ceremony was performed by Major Taliaferro.

On the 28th, Nicollet arrived from the Upper Mississippi.

On October 6, Inspector General Croghan, U. S. A., came to the Fort on an official visit, and the next night the Thespian Company played in his presence "Monsieur Tonson," and "the Village Lawyer."

On the 9th, a small steamboat came up with stores for the Government.

The following table will give some idea of the profits of the Indian trader in the year 1836:—

St. Louis prices.			Minnesota prices.				Net gain.	
Three pt. Blanket...	$3	25	60 Rat Skins at 20 cents,	$12	00		$8	75
1½ yd. Shroud........	2	37	60 " "		12	00	9	63
1 N. W. Gun........	6	50	100 " "		20	00	13	50
1 lb. Lead...........		6	2 " "			40		34
1 lb. Powder........		28	10 " "		2	00	1	72
1 Tin Kettle.........	2	50	60 " "		12	00	9	50
1 Knife		20	4 " "			80		60
1 lb. Tobacco........		12	8 " "		1	60	1	40
1 Looking Glass.....		4	4 " "			80		76
1½ yd. Scarlet Cloth..	3	00	60 " "		12	00	9	00

In the month of November a Mr. Pitt went with a boat and a party of men to the Falls of St. Croix to cut pine timber. The Chippeways gave the consent, but the agreement was not sanctioned by the United States authorities.

On Tuesday, the 29th of November, at the quarters of Capt. T. Barker, U. S. A., Alpheus R. French, of New York, was married to Mary Ann Henry, of Ohio.

On the 30th of December, there was an examination of the Mission School at Lake Harriet. Henry H. Sibley and Major Taliaferro were appointed examiners. Among others in attendance were Major Loomis, Lt. Ogden, and their families, and Surgeon Emerson.

In 1837 the Agent at Fort Snelling was instructed to organize a reliable delegation of Indians, to proceed to Washington, under orders from Gen. Henry Dodge, Superintendent of Indian Affairs, for the purpose of talking over the propriety of selling the lands owned by the Sioux east of the Mississippi. Miles Vineyard, sub-agent, was also dispatched to invite the Chippeways to a council near Fort Snelling, with the Commissioners, Gen. Wm. R. Smith, of Pa., and Gen. Dodge, of Illinois. In a little while 1200 Chippeways were at the Fort, to meet Gen. Dodge. A treaty was concluded, but not without some stirring incidents. Two prominent traders entered the Agency office in apparent haste, and asked for pens and paper. Some one returned and handed to Mr. Van Antwerp, Secretary of the Commissioner, a claim for the mills on the Chippeway River. The amount asked was $5000. The Indians were surprised at the palpable fraud. One chief, for the sake of peace, was willing to allow $500 for that which had been of no benefit to them, but old Hole-in-the-Day and others objected even to this.

Soon after yelling was heard in the direction of Baker's trading post at Cold Spring, and it was learned that Warren, the father of Wm. W. Warren, the Anglojibway that died at St. Paul several years ago, was marching down with some howling red devils to force the Commissioner to allow Warren $20,000. As they rushed into the treaty-arbor, Mr. Taliaferro pointed a pistol at Warren, and Hole-in-the-Day said, "Shoot, my father." Gen. Dodge begged him to stop, and the affair ended by the insertion of $20,000 in the treaty as Warren wished.

The treaty with the Chippeways being concluded, Gen. Dodge directed the Agent to select a delegation of Sioux and proceed to Washington.

The traders attempted to prevent the departure of the Sioux until they made a promise that they would provide for their indebtedness to the traders. The Agent, keeping his own counsel, engaged a steamboat to be at the landing on a certain day. Capt. Lafferty was prompt, and to the astonishment of the traders, the Agent, interpreters, and a part of the delegation were quickly on board, and gliding down the river. Stopping at Kaposia, they received Big Thunder and his pipe bearer; at Red Wing, Wahkoota and his war chief came aboard; and at Winona, Wapasha and Etuzepah were added, making in all a delegation of twenty-six.

Without accident they reached Washington, and a synopsis of a treaty that might be agreeable to the Indians was presented to Secretary Poinsett.

The Fur Company was there, represented by H. H. Sibley, Alexis Bailly, Laframboise, Rocque, Labathe, Alexander and Oliver Faribault; and on the 29th of September, 1837, a treaty was signed, by which the pine forests of the valley of the St. Croix and tributaries were rendered accessible to the white man, and thus a foundation laid for the organization of the future Territory of Minnesota.

The delegation returned by way of St. Louis, and the steamer Rolla was chartered to carry them back to Fort Snelling. On the trip one of the boilers collapsed, but fortunately no one was scalded, and on the 10th of November the party was landed in safety at the Fort.

On the 25th of May, 1838, the steamboat Burlington arrived with public stores. Among the passengers were J. N. Nicollet, J. C. Fremont and others, on an exploring expedition.

On June 9th, a delegation of Sioux from Kaposia came up to the Agency and complained that two men, Peter Parrant and old man Perry, had located on their lands east of the Mississippi, and wished them ordered away until the treaty was ratified. They also stated that Parrant (known to early settlers as Pigs' Eye) had located below the cave and sold whiskey.

On the 10th, Rev. Mr. Riggs of Lac-qui-parle preached to the troops at the Fort.

On the evening of the 13th, the steamboat Burlington, Captain Throckmorton, again arrived with a large number of passengers. Among others Capt. Maryatt, of the British Navy, and the popular novelist. Also, Gen. Atkinson and Lieut. Alexander, A. D. C., on a tour of inspection; Dr. and Mrs. Elwees, U. S. A., Benj. F. Baker, Franklin Steele, Miss Sibley, Miss E. B. Hooe, of Va., etc. The next day the whole party rode out to the Falls of St. Anthony.

On the 15th, the steamboat Brazil, Capt. Smith, was at the landing, and the then novel sight was presented of *two*

steamboats at the Fort at the *same time.*   The family of
Gov. Dodge came up on the latter.

On the 20th, the steamboat Ariel arrived from St. Louis,
and a Mr. Beebe, one of the passengers, said that the Senate
had ratified the treaty.

On the 28th, the Burlington completed its third trip this
season, and brought up 146 recruits for the 5th Infantry.

On the evening of 9th of July, there was a violent storm,
and as John B. Raymond, an old man sixty-five years of
age, was looking out from the door of Peter Quinn, near
Cold Water, he was instantly killed by lightning.   He
was buried in the graveyard of the Fort the next day.

The 15th of July was an eventful day at the Fort, caused
by the arrival of the Palmyra with an official notice of the
ratification of the treaty.

On board of the boat were some of the now old settlers
of Minnesota, who pitched their tents at Marine Mills and
the Falls of St. Croix.   Officers of the Fort and others also
now made claims at Prescott and Falls of St. Anthony.

On the 28th, Captain Boone, with fifty or sixty dragoons,
arrived from Fort Leavenworth, having been forty-five days
in making the journey, and in surveying the route for a
road from post to post.   Capt. Canfield, of the Topographical Engineers, and Lieut. Tilghman, were also members
of the Commission.

On the 2d of August, Hole-in-the-Day, who had killed
thirteen of the Lac-qui-parle Sioux, came to the Fort, with
a few Chippeways, much to the regret of the officer in command, Major Plympton.   The next evening Mr. Samuel W.
Pond met the Agent at Lake Harriet, and told him that a
number of armed Sioux, from Mud Lake, had gone to
Baker's trading house, to attack the Chippeways.   The
Agent immediately hastened toward the spot, and reached
the house just as the first gun was fired.   An Ottawa
Indian, of Hole-in-the-Day's party, was killed, and one

wounded. Of the Sioux, Tokali's son was shot by Obe-
quette, of Red Lake, just as he was scalping his victim.
The Chippeways were, as soon as possible, removed to the
Fort, and at nine o'clock at night one Sioux was confined
in the guard-house as a hostage.

The next day Major Plympton and the Indian Agent
determined to hold a council with the Sioux. The prin-
cipal men of the neighboring villages soon assembled.
Several long speeches, as usual, were made, when Major
Plympton said:—

"It is unnecessary to talk much. I have demanded the
guilty—they must be brought."

They replied they would. The Council broke up, and
at 5½ P. M. the party returned to the Agency, with Tokali's
two sons. With much ceremony they were delivered.
The mother, in surrendering them, said: "Of seven sons
three only are left; one of them was wounded, and soon
would die, and if the two now given up were shot, her all
was gone. I called on the head men to follow me to the
Fort. I started with the prisoners, singing their death-
song, and have delivered them at the gate of the Fort.
Have mercy on them for their youth and folly."

Notwithstanding the murdered Chippeway had been
buried in the graveyard of the Fort for safety, an attempt
was made on the night of the council, on the part of some
of the Sioux, to dig it up.

On the evening of the 6th, Major Plympton sent the
Chippeways across the river to the east side, and ordered
them to go home as soon as possible.

Major Plympton told the Sioux that the insult to the
flag must be noticed, and if they would punish the prisoners he would release them.

The council reassembled on the 8th, and Marcpuah Mah-
zali, Chief of Lake Pepin band, said, "If you will bring out
the prisoners, I will carry your views fully into effect."

Lieut. Whitehorne, officer of the day, was accordingly sent to bring the prisoners, and soon returned with them. The Chief then said:—

"We will not disgrace the house of my father. Let them be taken outside the enclosure." As soon as this was done his braves were called, and, amid the crying of the women, the prisoners were disgraced; their blankets were cut in small pieces, then their leggings and breech-cloths; after this their hair was cut off, and, finally, they were whipped with long sticks, a most humiliating infliction for a warrior to endure.

The affair being satisfactorily settled, the Indians quietly dispersed.

On the 16th of August, Franklin Steele, Mr. Livingston, and others, came around from the Falls of St. Croix in a barge. Jean N. Nicollet, with his assistants, Fremont and Geyer, returned to the post on the 25th, from explorations of the plains towards the Missouri.

Commissioners Pease and Ewing arrive in the steamboat Ariel, on the 27th, and sit as a board to examine half-breed claims and determine on alleged debts due the traders. Returning to St. Louis, the Ariel came back again on September 29th, with Indian goods, and $110,000 for the half-breed Sioux, and then made a trip up the St. Croix River.

Nicollet came back to the Fort from a second expedition this season, on the 17th of October.

Mrs. Perry came to the Agency on the 18th, and complained that the day before, some of Wapasha's band, at her house, just below the stone cave, now in the suburb of the city of St. Paul, attacked and killed three of her cattle. They did not like to see persons settle and prosper on lands that they had so recently ceded.

The Perry family were Swiss, who came down from Selkirk Settlement. The old man first settled near the Fort and became a great cattle raiser. As they constantly broke into the government gardens he was ordered away, but permitted to locate on the east side of the river. The ladies of the Fort did not wish him too far distant, as Mrs. Perry had distinguished herself in the region round about as an expert "*accoucheur.*" One of her daughters married James R. Clewett, and another was married to a man named Crevier.

The steamer Gipsy came up to the Fort on the 21st with Chippeway goods. For the sum of $450 it was then chartered to carry these goods to the Falls of St. Croix.

In passing up the lake, the boat grounded near the new town site, called Stambaughville, after the predecessor of Franklin Steele in the sutlership of Fort Snelling. On the afternoon of the 26th, the Falls were reached, and goods landed.

The increased arrival of steamboats in 1839, indicated that the country was in a transition state.

The first boat of the season was the Ariel, Captain Lyon, that reached the fort as early as April 14th. Twenty barrels of whiskey were brought in her for Joseph R. Brown, who had lived at Grey Cloud Island.

On May 2d the Gipsy, Captain Grey, came up, bringing a chaplain for the Fort, the Rev. E. G. Gear, who continued there until the post was disbanded.

The steamboat Fayette followed on the 11th, and after landing sutler's stores, proceeded with several persons of intelligence and character, connected with lumber companies, for the Falls of St. Croix.

On the 21st, the Glaucus, Captain Atchison, made its appearance. On its way it left six barrels of whiskey for D. Faribault, about the site of the city of St. Paul. The soldiers managed to obtain some and become mutinous, and many were put in the guard-house.

Years before this Mr. Faribault, sen., on one 22d of

February, is said to have received from Sergeant Mann $80 for a gallon of whiskey.

The Pennsylvania, Capt. Stone, arrived from Pittsburgh on June 1st, and among her passengers were Inspector General Wool and Major Hitchcock, both of whom have been in the service in crushing the present rebellion, with the rank of Major General.

The Glaucus made her second trip from St. Louis on the 5th of June.

The next day came the Ariel, bringing provisions for the Sioux.

On the 3d of June a party of soldiers went to Joseph R. Brown's groggery on the east side of the river, and as a consequence no less than forty-seven were confined in the guard-house that night for drunkenness.

On the afternoon of the 12th, Rev. Mr. Gavin, the Swiss missionary among the Sioux, was married to Miss C. Stevens, teacher of the Lake Harriet Mission School.

Hole-in-the-Day, father of the present chief of that name, arrived at the Fort with five hundred of his tribe on the 20th, and on the next day seven hundred and fifty more Chippeways came. At the same time there were eight hundred and seventy Sioux at the Agency. The steamboat Knickerbocker landed on the 25th and discharged goods for B. F. Baker, Sutler at the Post, and was followed on the next day by the Ariel, with stores for the Fur Company. Mr. Sinclair, of Selkirk settlement, with a train of forty or fifty carts, containing emigrants from the Red River of the North, encamped near the Fort on the 27th of June.

On board of the Ariel came a passenger by the name of Libley, who, in defiance of law, sold a barrel of whiskey to S. Campbell, U. S. Interpreter, and another to A. Leclerc. The result was that both Sioux and Chippeways were drunk the next night.

Bishop Loras of Iowa came up from Dubuque, and made

application to build a small Roman Catholic chapel near the Fort about this period.

On July 1st, the Swiss and Chippeways, at the Falls of St. Anthony, smoked the pipe of peace, and the latter proceeded homeward.

Some of the Pillager band of Chippeways remained behind, and passing over to Lake Harriet secreted themselves until after sunrise on July 2d, when they surprised Meekaw or Badger, a good Sioux Indian, on his way to hunt, and killed and scalped him. The Rev. J. D. Stevens of Lake Harriet brought the news to the Fort. The excitement was intense among the Sioux, and immediately one hundred and fifty warriors hurried after the Chippeways that had gone up the Mississippi, and another party soon followed after a second band of Chippeways, who with Mr. Aitkin had left the Fort the morning before to go to La Pointe by way of the St. Croix River.

On the 3d an action took place in the ravine near Stillwater, and also near Rum River portage. The losses of the Chippeways at the first place were twenty-one killed and twenty-nine wounded, and about ninety killed and wounded on Rum River.

The Rev. Thos. W. Pope, Methodist missionary, at Kaposia, left on the 16th, and was succeeded by the Rev. Jno. Holton.

Major Taliaferro now sent in his resignation as Indian Agent, to take effect at the close of the year.

The steamboat Ariel came up to the Fort on the 17th, and was followed by the Malta on the 22d, with the annuity goods for the Sioux. Among the passengers were Lt. Sibley, since Gen. Sibley of the rebel army, Lt. Marcy, now Inspector General U. S. A., with their families, Gen. Hunt and family, Mr. McCall of Philadelphia, and other gentlemen. The evening of the day of the arrival of the

Malta, at the quarters of Capt. A. S. Hooe, Mr. Bainbridge was married to Miss Hooe of Virginia.

On the 24th, the Malta went round to Lake St. Croix, for the passengers to visit the late battle ground in the ravine, where the Minnesota Penitentiary is now situated.

During the month of August the water in the river was so low that Louis Martin, the farmer for Grey Iron's band, drove his team down the bed of the river from the Fort to the trading post at Mendota.

Notwithstanding the low stage of water the light draught steamer Ariel reached the landing on the 15th of August.

A few days after this an order was received by Major Plympton defining the limits of the military reservation around Fort Snelling.

On the 8th of September some Sioux crossed over to the east side of the Mississippi and destroyed the groggery on the military reservation owned by Jos. R. Brown, Henry Mencke, a foreigner, and Anderson, a quarter breed Sioux.

The steamer Pike arrived on the 9th with ninety recruits, and again on the 17th with ninety-five more.

About the middle of September, an Irishman by the name of Hays was reported missing. He boarded with Phelan, in a log cabin near the junction of the present Hill and Eagle streets, in St. Paul, which was the second edifice erected on the site of the future capital of Minnesota.

As Hays had some money, and his absence was not satisfactorily accounted for by his partner Phelan, suspicion settled on the latter.

On the 22d of September Nicollet and Lt. J. C. Fremont arrived from Devil's Lake.

Some Indians came to the Agency on the 27th, and said that Hays, supposed to be lost, was dead and in the river near Carver's cave. The following note was received by the commanding officer of the Fort relative to the body:—

AGENCY HOUSE, ST. PETERS, Sept. 27, 1839.

MAJOR: I have sent the bearer, a good Indian, to go with the gentlemen who are in quest of the identity of Mr. Hays' body, now in the water near Carver's old cave. The Indian will conduct them to the spot, being so directed by his Chief, if requested so to do.

Very respectfully, your most ob't serv't,

LAW. TALIAFERRO, Indian Agent.

Major J. PLYMPTON, U. S. A. Comd'g Fort Snelling.

On examination of the body, his head, jaws, and nose were found fractured, indicating a violent death. The next day Phelan was brought before Henry H. Sibley, Justice of the Peace at Mendota, and examined as to his knowledge of the cause of the death of John Hays. He was confined in Crawford county prison for some time, but as there were no witnesses against him he was at last discharged, and coming back made a claim on the lake east of St. Paul, which to this day is called by his name.

On the 5th of October Henry C. Mencke, one of the whiskey sellers that prowled around on the east side of the river, having obtained an illegal appointment as special deputy sheriff for Clayton County, Iowa, went and arrested Major Taliaferro while sick, at the instance of one Clewett, on the false charge of aiding in destroying a whiskey cabin.

When the knowledge of this outrage reached the commanding officer, a detachment was sent over to Henry C. Mencke, who was an unnaturalized citizen as well as an intruder on the military reserve, and he was ordered to leave the country forthwith. The barefaced scamp, in arresting the Agent, surprised him in his morning dress, threw him on the floor, placed his knee on his stomach, and then presented a pistol to the Agent's ear.

On the 8th of October, the steamer Des Moines appeared with Indian goods.

The impudent conduct of the whiskey sellers between the Fort and the site of the present city of St. Paul, was made known to the War Department, but that very month Mr. Poinsett, then Secretary of Wisconsin, directed the U. S. Marshal of Wisconsin to remove all intruders on the land recently reserved for military purposes opposite to the post, on the east side of the river; and should they delay beyond a reasonable time, he was authorized to call upon the commander of the post for aid. All winter was given to the squatters to prepare, and the next spring there being a disposition to further procrastinate, on the 6th of May, 1840, the troops were called out, and the cabins destroyed to prevent re-occupation.

The squatters then retreated to the nearest point below the military reserve, and there they became the inglorious founders of a hamlet, which was shortly graced with the small Roman Catholic chapel of Saint Paul, the name of which is retained by the thrifty capital of Minnesota, which has emerged from the groggeries of "certain lewd fellows of the baser sort."

We could continue these reminiscences to the year of the organization of Minnesota, but there are many still living who are better acquainted with recent events than the writer, and he prefers to leave the task to some other pen.

www.ingramcontent.com/pod-product-compliance
Lightning Source LLC
Chambersburg PA
CBHW021443090426
42739CB00009B/1614